PILLOW TALK

"Roll Over and Face God"

Evangelist Shiela Austin Jones

xulon PRESS

Holiness Unto God Ministries (HUG) Ministries
P.O. Box 1432
Hammond, IN 46325-0874
(219) 931-9604 USA
Email: ptljones@juno.com

Edited by:
Heart to Heart Greetings
Hammond, IN 46407
e-mail: hearttoheartgreetings@yahoo.com

Front Cover Design by:
Byron Brazier, Jr.

www.xulonpress.com

Table of Contents

Acknowledgments
and Thank You

Thank You, God Jehovah and my precious Savior, Jesus Christ, for loving a sinner like me. I thought that drugs, alcohol and promiscuity was the answer. Yet, you died for me, knowing that one-day I would ask forgiveness of my sins, be filled with your Spirit, and become Your disciple. Thank you, Philip, my friend, my love, my husband, for your love and understanding during the many days I spend evangelizing. Thank you, Cecil Lampkins, Jr., my firstborn, my hero, who was always my support and protector during the hard times. Thank you, my beautiful daughter, my "roadrunner" partner, Tina Lampkins Robinson, for the many times you have arranged for me to get away and rest. Thank you, son number two, Chris Damyon Lampkins, my prayer partner and fellow laborer in the vineyard. You have always given me strength and courage to continue the race. Thank you, McDaniel Austin, Jr., "Macky," son number three for the many hours you spend time with me on the phone, sometimes listening to me repeat myself over and over. I thank you all for loving me in spite of all my failures.

I thank my pastor, Bishop Arthur M. Brazier, and Lady Isabel Brazier for their encouragement to strive for excellence in all I do for God. Thank you, Bishop E. Bobby Warren and Sis. Anita of Deliverance Temple C.O.G.I.C., for seeing potential in me even when I didn't.

Thank you, Mom and Dad, Raymond and Lillian McHenry, for love unconditional, taking us to church as children, and teaching us the importance of family. I thank my sisters: Loretta Hogans, who always inspires me to never give up; Ramona Jordan, who has always supported me unconditionally; Paula Respress, who strived with me until I surrendered to Christ (even buying me sharp outfits to wear for ministry); Janice Mardis Richards, who can find humor in every situation; and my baby sister, Della McHenry, now deceased, who always told me I was pretty. (Somehow she knew I needed to hear that.) I love you, Dell. I want to thank my only brother, Leroy McHenry, for opening his heart to Ricco. Ricco is my heart. I pray he'll always know how much I love him.

I also want to thank the following people: Mother Emma Mae Eckles, who has financially supported HUG ministry faithfully from the beginning; "Friends of HUG," from the bottom of my heart for your support; Dr. Mary Steele, for the spirit of excellence you have given to HUG; Goddaughter, Ernestine (Shanta) Jeffers, a mighty woman of faith, my fellow partner in evangelizing the "world"; Patsy Laurant, for being a faithful friend and traveling companion for more than thirty years; Minister Dedra Tucker, an anointed intercessor who always has a fresh Rhema word to prophetically speak into my life; Minister Genetra Hickson of Heart to Heart Greeting Cards for your perseverance and patience in helping to edit this book; Minister Marilyn Bell, for your ministry blessing our seniors; and my spiritual daughter, Princess Lugrash "Cookie" White, for your sweet spirit that changes the atmosphere wherever we are; and thank you, Judy Scott, for the sweet fellowship only a friend can give.

I thank many fellow laborers in the gospel, too numerous to name, for interceding and speaking words of life into the ministry God gave me. People like Dartania, Mary, Duane, Karen, Shirley & Al, Sis. Tolliver, Charlene, Sylvia "Teeter." I love you! How could I not thank my friends like Ellen Jane, Gladys, Amelia, Donna, and those of you who have been there since childhood? To Archie Waits, Beverly Pitchford, and Leroy Norwood; thanks for always going that extra mile.

I must thank God for my grandchildren: Makisha, Monika, Crystal, Cecilia, Tina Marie, Chris, Jr. (A mighty man of valor now in heaven.), Jeremiah Brent, and Londo'n; and my great grandchildren: Majesty Grace, Josiah Daquan, and Destiny. I am leaving out a special mention of many who are dear to my heart. You may have thought I forgot you. Well, I haven't. I just have to stop. My true friends will understand and forgive me; others who don't I guess were only a friend for a season. Sincerely know that any name omitted was not intentional.

Foreword

"And they overcame him by the blood of the Lamb,
and by the word of their testimony."

Revelation 12:11a (KJV)

This Scripture epitomizes this book. It is a blessing to know that God has given Evangelist Jones a powerful testimony and she is not afraid to share it.

Having read this book and her previous book, *Made Whole In The Potters Hand,* I see that Shiela has learned what so many of us are still struggling to believe: "All things work together for our good" (Romans 8:28). Had she not endured the trials and struggles that were placed before her, so many of us would not know that we, too, could make it.

This book touches on the very heart of God to set us free. "He who the Son sets free is free indeed!" Yet we must be truthful to ourselves about which horse we are riding in order to dismount and never ride it again. "We must know the truth and the truth will set us free!" Amen, Hallelujah! Shiela has so gracefully outlined the truth in this book.

Whether you are riding the "rocking horse," "wild horse," "show horse," "race horse," or "horse drawn carriage," the blood of Jesus is the way of escape.

Thank you, Shiela, for once again baring your soul for the sake of others. Deliverance is the children's bread, and if we say we are the children of God, we can eat freely at the table. Eat on, my sisters and brothers. Write on, Shiela!

— Evangelist Pamela "Brenda" Little

CHAPTER 1

Intimacy Revisited

I have never been so impressed with the relationship God demands of His people. I realize my hunger and thirst for righteousness comes from drawing closer and closer to a holy God. The more I love Him, the more I want to remain in His presence. The more I remain in His presence, the more it becomes clear that there are areas of my flesh still needing to be crucified.

In a day and age where everyone is looking for someone to love and to be loved, my God is wooing me to fall head over heels in love with Him. Jesus wants me to become so close in our relationship that He means more to me than I mean to myself. He means more to me than all my bills being paid. He means more to me than all my family being saved. He means more to me than my body being healed!

If we could just have some pillow talk! You remember when we had slumber parties where we talked about our innermost secrets? We told secrets to our best friend that we didn't tell anyone else. Yet some of those same friends are not even in our lives today. Some of those friends turned out to not be friends after all. Some of those friends betrayed our friendship.

Jesus is saying, "Shiela, roll over, face Me. I am a friend who sticks closer than a brother. I will never tell your secrets; I already know them. I will never leave you or betray you. I want intimacy that you've never had with another. I will never misuse your love or take it for granted."

I say, "Yes, Jesus, let's talk about the past, the present, and the future. Let me pour out my feelings, hurts, longings, and desires. Let me lie in your bosom and share my innermost feelings. Let me have the closest relationship with you that I could ever have with another. Let me have intimacy I've never known with another. I long for pillow talk!"

Jesus says, "Roll over and face Me. See how much I have longed to spend this time with you. Look in my eyes and see how much I love you. See my compassion, my forgiveness, my grace, and my mercy. Face Me!"

"Lord, here I am. Let our relationship become stronger than ever before!"

Jeremiah 29:11-14 says,

"For I know the plans I have for you." Declares the LORD, "plans to prosper you and not to harm you, plans to give you hope and a future. Then you will call upon Me, and you will come and pray to Me, and I will hear and heed you. Then you will seek Me, inquire for, and require Me [as a vital necessity] and find Me when you search for Me with all your heart. I will be found by you, says the Lord, and I will release you from captivity and gather you from all the nations and all the places to which I have driven you, says the Lord, and I will bring you back to the place from which I caused you to be carried away captive.

AMP

Yes, this Scripture is talking to the people of Israel, the Jews, when they were in captivity in Babylon. How hard it must have been to be in a land where people didn't worship God, and how easy it would have been to think all the non-believers told you was true. Or better yet, you might find it easier to "go along with the program." It would be so much easier to act like one of them and not let anyone know you have a personal relationship with a true and living God. It is like today, when every place we turn we are being told that if we aren't rich, or if we haven't been healed, or if our children are still on drugs, we don't have faith in our God. If bad things are happening to us, we must not be living right, or we must have some sin in our lives. Yet everywhere there is life there are good people who love God, who have faith, and who are still suffering. All through the Bible we read of our favorite disciples who suffered much more than we have. Some were killed by the sword, boiled in oil, crucified upside down, beheaded, etc. Were they not in God's favor?

My, what hope I receive from this passage of Scripture when God speaks to my spirit and says, "I know the plans I have for you, plans for welfare and not for evil, to give you an expected end!" Please know that even if you are in despair, never believe the hype! Even when God caused the Jews to be in captivity, Jeremiah told them that even in captivity, they could be blessed. I am convinced that if God allows bad things to happen to us, He will surely bring us out and it all will work for our good! Let's face it, we live in a sinful world and it rains on the just and the unjust!!!

The key is to get to a place in God where nothing matters but our intimacy with Him; a place where we truly seek Him with our whole heart; a place where we can tell him our innermost thoughts and dreams on our pillow at night; a place where we gain strength in the comfort of His words.

One night while at the Monday evening Women of Power fellowship, I was talking to my friend, Evangelist

Pam Little. She blessed me with a testimony of lying on her bed for hours in anguish. Going through a tremendous test, she was praying and asking God how much longer it would be before the pain went away. Finally, she got to a point in her need for God where she asked, "God, where are You?" She said she heard Him say, "I'm right here, roll over." She stated she rolled over and a bright, peaceful presence had filled her room. She described the exact intimacy God wants with us. The Scripture says He will bring you back to a place from which He caused you to be taken captive. If He caused it, you've got to keep your focus on the fact that He has a plan! What better person to trust our lives with, than a person who never half finishes a project? What He has started, He will finish.

I like to think of us as riding horses in different stages of life. Since the mode of transportation in most of the Bible days contained horses, my imagination goes to horses. I have a great imagination, and it can be a comfort to those of us who have been through any trauma. If you were a product of incest, rape, verbal, physical, or mental abuse, you know how easy it is to escape with imagination. You can imagine you are in some other place than the place where the pain is being perpetrated. You can imagine you are some great person rather than the person you consider yourself to be.

I remember when I was a child I used to imagine being Bette Davis, playing a role as a crazy person. I'd pick up a butcher knife while doing dishes with siblings. I'd then put on the ugliest face and draw the knife as if to attack them. When they ran out of the house in fear, it made me feel good. I felt in control. Even though I knew I'd get a beating when my parents got home, it was worth it to be someone else. (Yep, I had issues!)

When I look back on my early adult life—going to modeling school, working on my outward appearance—I still enjoyed pretending to be someone else. Even singing in nightclubs, traveling with the band, I had to get high on drugs or alcohol to portray some singer. Only intimacy with Jesus Christ, and realizing who you are in Him and what **He** thinks of you, changes you into loving who you are, once you become born again. You are a child of the King, joint heirs with Jesus Christ! Your past abuse, your present circumstance, or your future disappointments will not change who you are in Christ!

Let me get back to the horses. Things we see affect us in different ways. When my children saw my ex-husband abusing me, each was affected in different ways. One day their father had a razor to my neck against a wall in the bathroom of our house on Altgeld Street in Chicago, Illinois. The baby at the time, Chris, around four years old, beat on his dad's legs, begging him not to kill me. That was his reaction. Tina, my only girl, around 6 years old, went into hysterics, screaming and crying; that was her reaction. Cecil, our hero, around 7 years old, was always the one who felt he had to take care of us. Even as he got older, he got a job and was always responsible. His reaction to the circumstance at hand was to run back into the kitchen, get a knife from the drawer, and protect us. When his dad saw the knife, he took the razor from my throat, left the bathroom, and picked up the chair to protect himself. At that point we were all in the bathroom and had shut the door, petrified that he would break the door down. God had other plans for my life and the lives of my children. Otherwise, we would not be here today. Think about your life. Quit bellyaching over the past and be thankful for the character-building taking place in your life through every trial and test. You may not feel it while you are going through, but God is building character with every disappointment.

When we are involved in violence or our children see fighting among their parents, there is an effect that takes place that only intimacy with Jesus Christ can heal. There are many shelters for you to go for refuge when there is physical abuse in the house. Too many people think they have no way out. Women have shared with me that they are afraid to leave. Not only because of the abusive relationship, but they are afraid of losing their man. I am telling you women to get intimate with the real man. The man who loves you so much He died for you even though you were a sinner! The only man who can heal that relationship, deliver your mate from the anger, and make you whole! Jesus Christ is His name. Go to a shelter while your mate gets counseling. Stop the drama before it escalates. Don't be ashamed and don't feel guilty. Anger must be dealt with! It cannot be pushed under the rug.

Let's let that go for now and look at chapter seven of the book of Acts. Stephen, the first martyr, had reminded the nation about their persistent rejection of God, even called them stiff-necked (v. 51) and ended up being cast out of the city and stoned (v. 53). Do you know that there had to be a real intimate relationship with Jesus Christ for him to have been stoned for the cause of Christ? Look at vv. 55, 59, and 60:

> "But he, being full of the Holy Ghost, looked up steadfastly into heaven, and saw the glory of God, and Jesus standing on the right hand of God, and said, "Behold, I see the heavens opened and the Son of man standing on the right hand of God". And they stoned Stephen, calling upon God, and saying, Lord Jesus, receive my spirit. And he kneeled down, and cried with a loud voice, Lord; lay not this sin to their charge. And when he had said this, he fell sleep."
> Wow! Now that's intimacy!

On the other hand, in verse 58 we find mention of a young man whose name was Saul. The witnesses of the stoning laid down their garments at Saul's feet. Saul, who had watched all this abuse, had watched this hatred and saw a murder. Do you think it affected his reaction to Christianity? I feel it had to have so much of an effect that it caused a reaction in Saul to persecute, to see people suffer, to kill and throw people into prison. Your reaction to violence is different when there is no personal relationship with Jesus Christ. Saul did not know Jesus. He knew religion. There is a big difference. Religious people ride a rocking horse.

CHAPTER 2

The Rocking Horse

~~

"Saul made havoc of the church entering into every house and haling men and women committing them to prison."

Acts 8:3

"And he fell to the earth and heard a voice saying Saul, Saul, why persecuteth thou me?"

Acts 9:4

I'd like to use my imagination regarding Saul of Tarsus. Saul was full of religion and so sure his way was the right way. He was riding a rocking horse back and forth, back and forth. He had to be full of anger, blinded by hatred, and frustration. Saul probably thought, "Why did Stephen allow himself to be stoned for this 'Jesus' gospel? Doesn't he know the Scriptures? Doesn't he know the letters?" Acts 9:1-2 (NIV) says,

"Meanwhile, Saul was still breathing out murderous threats against the Lord's disciples. He went to the high priest and asked him for letters to the synagogues in Damascus, so that if he found any there who belonged to the Way, whether men or women, he might take them as prisoners to Jerusalem."

Saul was persecuting Christians and persecuting someone's husband, wife, daughter, or son. He had to be full of anger! You can't have that much hatred without anger. That is why so many of our homes are filled with abuse. So many "churchgoers" have no intimate relationship with Jesus Christ, and only intimacy with Him can heal us from past experiences and deliver us from the anger!

Until Saul was knocked onto the ground and blinded, he thought he was doing God a favor. He even got society's approval, a seal to condone his behavior. Then something happened that changed everything! Acts 9:3-9 (NIV) says,

"As he neared Damascus on his journey, suddenly a light from heaven flashed around him. He fell to the ground and heard a voice say to him, "Saul, Saul, why do you persecute me? "Who are you, Lord?" Saul asked. "I am Jesus, whom you are persecuting," he replied. "Now get up and go into the city, and you will be told what you must do."

The men traveling with Saul stood there speechless; they heard the sound but did not see anyone. Saul got up from the ground, but when he opened his eyes he could see nothing. So they led him by the hand into Damascus. For three days he was blind, and did not eat or drink anything.

No matter what God has to do to us to complete the plan for our lives, He will do it! The Bible goes on to say that God chose a man called Ananias, who heard of Saul's reputation, to witness to Saul! In verse 15, Jesus speaks to Ananias and says, "Go! This man is my chosen instrument to carry my name before the Gentiles and their kings and before the people of Israel. I will show him how much he must suffer for my name." Why would God choose a person who persecuted His followers? He has such a sense of humor!

Can it be that God uses sinners like me to bless His people? A woman who smoked drugs, drank alcohol, committed fornication? A woman who lied and treated people badly? Could people who we have branded "castaways" be God's chosen? What does the phrase "born again" mean? I can witness that it means you truly become a new creature! Old things are passed away, and all things become new! How can I talk about the old me? How can I share with the world what I did? I thank God that person is dead and I am alive in Christ, born again, brand new!

On the ground that day, I imagine that Saul had to turn and face God. Only then did his life change. His eyes were opened naturally and spiritually, and his intimate relationship with Jesus began.

Pillow talk is an intimate relationship that produces intimate conversation with the one who loves us best and will never tell our secrets. Someone who we can trust wholeheartedly. Someone who won't quit loving us the moment we do something that does not please Him. Someone who suffered and died while we were yet sinners. Romans 5:8 says, "But God commended his love toward us, in that, while we were yet sinners, Christ died for us."

I used to find myself riding life, rocking back and forth, full of anger from past abuse, going nowhere, full of religion. I was a churchgoer. I sang in the choir, played the piano for the choir, and was still full of lust. Would you believe that I went to quartet concerts to pick out which guy I'd leave the church with? I was still partying, getting high, and thinking I was doing okay because I had no intimate relationship with Jesus Christ. I was rocking back and forth, back and forth. There was lots of movement, but I was going nowhere. When I look back on how I used to be, I wonder how Jesus could have loved me so much! He died for me, knowing all my sins. He had a plan, and I'm in that plan! It's for good and not evil!

Our world is full of churches with members still riding high on abuse. Did you know that there are husbands in the pulpit beating their wives at home? You right now could be riding a rocking horse full of pride. You could be riding cocaine and alcohol, backbiting, adultery, homosexuality— "if it feels good, do it." If so, you are riding a horse that's taking you nowhere. You go to church empty and leave church empty if you are not taught the gospel of Jesus Christ and accept Him as your personal Savior. It's time to dismount the rocking horse!

God's love is steadfast, waiting patiently for us to get tired of our way. When God saved me, I became born again. He changed my mind, my way of thinking. Ephesians 4:22-24 (NIV) says,

> "You were taught, with regard to your former way of life, to put off your old self, which is being corrupted by its deceitful desires; to be made new in the attitude of your minds and to put on the new self, created to be like God in true righteousness and holiness."

Can you believe that the same lustful person I was could become a chaste woman of God? After being filled with the Holy Ghost, I had to be taught how to be complete in Jesus. Jesus plus 1 equals a whole! I was a divorcee for more than fifteen years. During the fifteen-plus years, while also a single parent, God molded me into a person complete "in the beloved." Colossians 2:8-10 says,

> "Beware lest any man spoil you through philosophy and vain deceit, after the tradition of men, after the rudiments of the world and not after Christ. For in

Him dwells all the fullness of the Godhead bodily. And you are complete in him, which is the head of all principality and power."

While riding the rocking horse, I was looking for satisfaction in all the wrong places. My heart now pants after God. Psalms 42:1, 2a says,

"As the hart panteth after the water brooks, so panteth my soul after thee, O God. My soul thirsts for God, for the living God."

I hear God saying: "Roll over, face me. Call Me—pray to Me. I will hear you; My thoughts are good, not evil, and will give you an expected end."

CHAPTER 3

The Wild Horse

Maybe you're not riding a rocking horse. Possibly you've been born again. You've accepted Jesus as your personal Savior. You've confessed your sins, and He has been faithful and just and forgiven you of your sins. If you have done this and still want your own way about your life, you may be riding a wild horse! If you're reading this book and think you don't need to admit you are a sinner and need Jesus as your Lord, then I guarantee you are riding a wild horse. If you are looking at believers, who have changed their way of living to a sanctified walk with Jesus, and you are thinking "it doesn't take all that," then I can personally tell you that you are riding a wild horse! If you are a born again believer and have been saved for ten years, still sitting in the pew while criticizing everyone else who is doing something for God, you should examine yourself. Are you riding a wild horse?

What does a wild horse do? It bucks everything. That is why it is sometimes called an ass or a donkey—stubborn! Jonah 1:1-9 (NIV) says,

"The word of the LORD came to Jonah son of Amittai:
"Go to the great city of Nineveh and preach against
it, because its wickedness has come up before me."

But Jonah ran away from the LORD and headed for
Tarshish. He went down to Joppa, where he found a
ship bound for that port. After paying the fare, he went
aboard and sailed for Tarshish to flee from the LORD.

Then the LORD sent a great wind on the sea, and
such a violent storm arose that the ship threatened to
break up. All the sailors were afraid and each cried
out to his own god. And they threw the cargo into the
sea to lighten the ship.

But Jonah had gone below deck, where he lay down
and fell into a deep sleep. The captain went to him and
said, "How can you sleep? Get up and call on your
god? Maybe he will take notice of us, and we will not
perish."

Then the sailors said to each other, "Come, let us cast
lots to find out who is responsible for this calamity"
They cast lots and the lot fell on Jonah.

So they asked him, "Tell us, who is responsible for
making all this trouble for us? What do you do?
Where do you come from? What is your country?
From what people are you?"

He answered, "I am a Hebrew and I worship the LORD,
the God of heaven, who made the sea and land."

Can you imagine how this sounds? How can you be a true
worshipper of this great God who made heaven and earth and

all that dwells therein and run from His plan for your life? If He rules the heavens and the earth, surely we can allow Him full course over our life! Verse 10 says, "This terrified them and they asked, 'What have you done?'" They knew he was running away from the Lord, because he had already told them so.

God said, "Go to Nineveh." Verse 3 says that Jonah ran from God. How can we run from a God who is omnipresent? Verse 12 says, "'Pick me up and throw me into the sea,' Jonah replied, 'and it will become calm. I know that it is my fault that this great storm has come upon you.'" The men had to throw Jonah overboard, and Jonah was willing to die rather than obey God! This sort of reminds me of people taking drugs, having sex without the benefit of marriage, and risking dying rather than obeying God. It's like attempting to ride a wild horse without first experiencing the discomfort and patience required to tame and prepare that horse! Stubborn! Listen, if God has to provide a big fish to swallow you up to get your attention, so be it! Jonah 1:17 says, "But the LORD provided a great fish to swallow Jonah, and Jonah was inside the fish three days and three nights."

A wild horse doesn't think of anything other than how uncomfortable he is. Jonah was being asked to come out of his comfort zone! "I'm going to Tarshish." The Bible says Jonah paid a fare to go to Tarshish. What a price to pay when we ride the bucking wild horse instead of coming out of our comfort zone! It's not always that what we're doing is wrong, it's that God told us to do something else.

We tell God, "I'm tired of being single!"

God says, "Wait, delight in Me, and I will give you your heart's desire."

"But I want what I want, and everyone else is doing it!"

"But he belongs to another woman."

"But he looks so good, and he said he was going to leave her and marry me."

God says, "My child, I love you too much to give you a married man." What dialogue!

I overheard one woman in a testimony service saying God showed her her next husband before she was divorced! I'd like to ask you this: if God ordained marriages and hates divorce, would He show you someone else when you are already married? God is about healing relationships, not having us dismiss them and go to the next one like we do a new pair of shoes! Quit riding a wild horse and being too stubborn to work out the differences and pray for your mate.

Remember David and Bathsheba? During the time David was lusting after Uriah's wife, he was riding a wild horse. He was bucking against the will of God! He was entertaining the thoughts of his flesh over the anointing of God on his life. First Corinthians 10:13 says, "There hath not temptation taken you but such as is common to man: but God is faithful, who will not suffer you to be tempted above that you are able; but will with the temptation also make a way to escape, that you may be able to bear it."

2 Samuel 11:2-4 says,

> And it came to pass in an evening tide, that David arose from his bed, and walked upon the roof of the king's house: and from the roof he saw a woman washing herself and the woman was very beautiful to look upon. And David sent and inquired after the woman. And one said, Is not this Bathsheba, the daughter of Eliam, the wife of Uriah the Hittite?

> And David sent messengers, and took her; and she came in unto him, and he lay with her; for she was purified from her uncleanness: and she returned unto her house."

Ever wonder why Satan always makes us think we can sin and get away with it? You cannot sin and cover it up! God sees and knows all things. What is done in the dark will come into the light!

When we read further in 2 Samuel, we find that David's lust led to adultery, adultery led to lies, and lies led to murder. All because he listened to the flesh instead of trusting God. There is always that still, small voice inside of every believer, leading and guiding us. But when we refuse to listen to that voice, we find ourselves making a mess of our lives. Yet God says His plans for us are good and not evil. When we mess up, we have to ask forgiveness and be thankful that God doesn't change His mind because of our human frailties.

I guess you might say I found myself trying to help God with my life. I remember when I first repented of my sins and asked God into my life. I decided I'd better hurry and get married. After all, I felt I had to have a boyfriend, and since fornication was sin, wouldn't it be God's will for me to hurry and marry? So I told God the first man who mentioned Him before I did would be the one. We make so many deals with God as baby saints because we haven't learned to trust Him. I'd been in sin so long; I did not know that this great God who had saved me could be trusted to keep me!

Anyway, I went down south to a funeral with my Grandma Young. One evening as I walked from my cousin's kitchen into her living room, I saw a really handsome man sitting on her couch. He asked me if I was the one singing on the tape he was listening to. I told him I was. He said, "You really have a gift from God; make sure you always use it for Him."

I hope I can excuse myself for being so naïve, since I was a "newborn" saint, but I took this to be an excuse for marrying this man. I took it as a "sign" and went into one of the bedrooms and looked up at the ceiling and said, "Praise God, he must be the one." Listen, I know you're laughing at me, but I have since heard some crazy testimonies from other believers who have done some of the same stupid things. (Smile.)

This handsome guy wrote me sweet letters after I went back home. We talked on the phone constantly. Within a couple of months, he came to Indiana, found a job, and we got married. Almost two years later, we had a beautiful son and named him Macky. This was the most beautiful outcome of this relationship: a handsome, intelligent son. This part of my life was working for my good because I loved God and was called according to His purpose.

The marriage relationship was not good. He was a deacon in the church, but he had never had a born again experience with Jesus Christ and was not saved. He was riding that rocking horse I talked about in another chapter. The whole relationship had been built on lies. His cousin had written the letters I thought he had written me during our courtship! Also, he was a bigamist, having been married when he was a teenager and never divorced.

He wanted to make our marriage legal by divorcing and remarrying. By then I knew I had made a terrible mistake by trying to show God how to keep my flesh under subjection to the spirit man. I had to know God for myself and surrender my fleshly desires to Him. I had to trust Him to deliver me just like He delivered me from the desire for cigarettes, drugs, and alcohol. I began to pray more, fast, and read my Bible more. I asked God to show me what to do. When I didn't hear an answer, I did what we should always do while waiting on God to answer. Be content to live in the state you're in through prayer, supplication, and thanksgiving. God answered my request. My "husband" made a decision to leave and returned to his hometown. I made a decision to be legally divorced even though not legally married.

Now look at my situation. I now had four kids instead of three and was still single but more mature in the Lord. I was no longer bucking against the will of God. I was no longer taking things into my own hands and trying to "help" God fix my situation. It looks like I dismounted from the wild horse I was riding and decided to roll over and face God!!

God can do anything but fail! For more than fifteen years, until I was almost fifty years old, God proved over and over that He is a keeper. I desired to be celibate until marriage because God's Word said so. The miracle of it was my relationship with God was so precious that I got to the point that if I never married it would be okay, just as long as I was in the will of God. How could a woman go from thinking she couldn't live without a man to a woman who was changed so completely? Only a "new creature" in Christ brings about the difference. 2 Corinthians 5:17 says,

"Therefore if any man be in Christ, he is a new creature: old things are passed away; behold all things are become new."

By the way, God's plan for me was marriage. Six months before my fiftieth birthday, I was married to a beautiful spirit-filled man of God who still holds me in his arms and prays for me before I leave to go out evangelizing. I thank God for my husband and the support he gives me in the ministry. God's plans are of good, and not evil to give an expected end.

In another example of a wild horse, God may tell you, "Hold on to your marriage." You may say, "I'm tired of waiting, tired of holding on to past promises, past prophecies, tired of forgiving over and over again!" You may even get to the point where you feel you don't love your spouse anymore.

God says, "Keep praying for your husband or wife. I hate divorce; don't put asunder what I have put together." You keep bucking, giving God excuse after excuse as if God doesn't know everything. He hears the verbal abuse you may suffer. He wants you to be so intimate with Him that you will be able to hear Him say sweet things in your ear to drown out that ugly abuse.

While you're listening to God, let God deal with that ugly demonic force by using you through prayer. You can't pray effectively when you are involved and hurt or screaming back at the ugly spirit. Keep your mind free from having to answer back by hearing God's voice. When you have your hand on your hip and your finger waving, you are playing right into the same ugly spirit. You can stay "cool" when you know that nothing that person says to you can change who God knows you are. The same way God changed you, He can change them. Quit riding that wild horse and pray! We wrestle not with flesh and blood but spiritual wickedness in high places!!

I have heard about many women who have gotten so fed up with the harsh words spoken to them by their spouses, they leave. They are married to men full of anger, and the anger is taken out on the wife through verbal abuse. I want those women to remember God has a plan, and His plan has an expected end. Remember who you are in God's eyes! You will not have a problem when you know that what someone says to you in anger does not change who you are, nor does it change God's plans.

When you keep your focus, the right spirit will put you in a position where you don't take it personally. When you take what is said in anger personally, you are too upset to pray. The devil then has two of you on his side! Keep your mind on God and His plans for your life and what He says about you, so you can pray. God says you are the head and not the tail. God says you are more than a conqueror. Leave your feelings out of it so you can pray. When a woman prays, God makes things happen! Soon you will begin to see a change in your mate! Quit bucking! Roll over, face God, HE has a plan.

Can you see yourself riding a wild horse at church? Bucking against coming out of your comfort zone? What about when your pastor says, "Lead the praise service"? Do you say, "I can't sing good enough." What about if you are asked to become an usher? Do you answer, "That's not my calling"? God allows our pastors to see potential in us we can't see in ourselves, and instead of us being obedient we buck! Buck! (I guess I shouldn't mention paying tithes and offerings.)

God is saying to us, "Roll over and face Me! Look into My eyes and see you can trust Me. Let Me fill the void in your life. If you're single, give Me your loneliness and emptiness." Being married does not fulfill that void. Ask your married sisters! Some of them are more lonely even with their husband lying beside them! No human being can fill that void! Only God can fill it. A wild horse must be broken. Quit bucking! Let God break you!"

Luke 3:5-6 says, "Every valley shall be filled and every mountain and hill shall be brought low, and the crooked shall be made straight, and the rough ways shall be made smooth: and all the flesh shall see the salvation of God."

Let me get back to Jonah. Jonah 2:1-9 says,

From inside the fish Jonah prayed to the LORD, his God. He said: "In my distress I called to the LORD, and he answered me. From the depths of the grave I called for help, and you listened to my cry. You hurled me into the deep, into the very heart of the seas, and the currents swirled about me; all your waves and breakers swept over me.

I said, 'I have been banished from your sight; yet I will look again toward your holy temple.' The engulfing waters threatened me, the deep surrounded me; seaweed was wrapped around my head. To the roots of the mountains I sank down; the earth beneath barred me in forever. But you brought my life up from the pit, O LORD my God. "When my life was ebbing away, I remembered you, LORD, and my prayer rose to you, to your holy temple. "Those who cling to worthless idols forfeit the grace that could be theirs.

But I, with a song of thanksgiving, will sacrifice to you. What I have vowed I will make it good. Salvation comes from the LORD."

Can you imagine a prayer like that? Look at how God will answer you when you quit "bucking" against His plans: "And the LORD commanded the fish, and it vomited Jonah onto dry land." Jonah had to roll over and face God while in the belly of the fish! Jonah dismounted and decided to obey God. Jonah decided to dismount the wild horse and found intimacy with God. He rolled over and faced God's plan for his life!!

CHAPTER 4

The Show Horse

A show horse loves to prance! In the book of Esther we learn of Ahasuerus, king of Persia. Esther 1:1,3,4 says,

> "Now it came to pass in the days of Ahasuerus, (this is Ahasuerus which reigned, from India even unto Ethiopia, over an hundred and seven and twenty provinces), In the third year of his reign, he made a feast unto all his princes and his servants; the power of Persia and Media, the nobles and princes of the provinces, being before him, When he showed the riches of his glorious kingdom and the honor of his excellent majesty many days, even an hundred and fourscore days."

In other words, this king partied 120 days bragging about his riches and seven additional days where everyone was drinking the royal wine out of gold vessels. On the seventh day, King Ahasuerus called for Queen Vashti (his favorite show piece) to parade before him with the crown of royal!

Vashti, in the meantime, had her own feast for the maidens in the royal house. Esther 1:9 says, "Also Vashti the queen made a feast for the women in the royal house which belonged to King Ahasuerus."

Can you use your imagination? Think about Vashti's maidens. You can almost hear them saying, "Girl, I wish I were you! You got it made with all your pretty clothes, being bathed in the best oils, and having everyone waiting on you. Girl, you really got it goin' on! Man oh man, if I could only be queen for one day!" I imagine Queen Vashti may have been riding a show horse.

A show horse is all pretty on the outside, but it hides all the pain on the inside. The maidens didn't realize that even though Vashti was the king's prized possession, she wasn't complete. She knew one day she would be replaced by a younger woman. She knew one day lines and sagging would become a part of her looks. She knew that though life looked good, nothing she had belonged to her. Her clothes, jewelry, and even the oils she bathed in all belonged to the king. I imagine Queen Vashti may have been thinking about all this the day she was called for by the king.

Esther 1:10-12 (NIV) says,

"On the seventh day, when King Xerxes was in high spirits from wine, he commanded the seven eunuchs who served him, to bring before him Queen Vashti, wearing her royal crown, in order to display her beauty to the people and nobles, for she was lovely to look at. But when the attendants delivered the king's command, Queen Vashti refused to come. Then the king became furious and burned with anger."

Think about it. When Queen Vashti refused to come at the king's command, she took a chance on giving up her livelihood, her prestige, her "rank." I like to think she decided to dismount the show horse rolled over and faced God. At that moment she saw she was more than just a showpiece. She began to get her self-respect back. God's plans for her were for good to give her an expected end!

Do you feel as though you have a Vashti mentality? Do you think so low of yourself that you feel you have no other use than to be man's showpiece; feeling pretty on the outside, hiding all the pain on the inside? Do you have men pawing you and making lewd remarks? Do you find yourself dressing sexy to keep the attention coming? Are men giving you money to "help with the children"? (I remember using this as an excuse, before my relationship with Jesus Christ. I remember telling myself I needed the money from my boyfriends to "help with the kids." In reality, I liked the gifts they would buy. In reality, I needed a Savior.) I also felt I was using them in revenge for the abuse I suffered from other men. I dressed in a way that was not pleasing to God, because this is what we do when we are not filled with the Holy Spirit. A "show horse" longs for the wrong kind of attention.

I heard one preacher say that when you show the public everything, you carry with you a message that you are willing to share it with everyone. Proverbs 31:30 says,

"Charm is deceitful and beauty is vain, but a woman who fears the Lord is to be praised."

Again, I imagine that on the day Queen Vashti refused the king, she rolled over and faced God. She saw herself as she was in God's eyes and decided it was time to make a change. Her intimate relationship with God began! What pillow talk she and Jesus might have had to give her strength to dismount the "show horse" mentality!

After I became born again, my thoughts changed. Even though I was still a divorcee with four children, God was teaching me how special I was to Him. One day I received a great message in my spirit. The message was sort of like a vision. In the vision I was reminded of how when I am in an ordinary store and try on cheap jewelry, no one seems to mind. I pick it up off the counter, try it on, and throw it back on the counter. If I wish to purchase this cheap jewelry, I may even have to look for a sales clerk to wait on me. However, in a very exclusive jewelry store like Tiffany's, if I see a very expensive piece of jewelry that costs thousands, I must ask the owner to make it available to me. He then goes to the safe, gets the key, unlocks the glass case, pulls out the box, uses the key to open the box, and carefully places the jewelry in my hand. He watches me very closely because the piece of jewelry is very rare and can't easily be found. It's been intricately cut and molded for a specific person willing to pay the price for it.

Before God will let anyone handle you, His most prized possession, they will have to go to the "Master" for the key. Remember, God's plans are of good and not evil. They are "to give you a future and a hope," and He's not about to give the key to anyone who is unworthy of you. Jesus paid an awesome price for you when He gave His life. You are not your own!

Can you imagine Jesus saying to you; "Roll over, face Me… Surrender your crown, and I'll make you my queen… Cover up your outward appearance to stand naked before Me. Stand naked before Me and I'll clothe you with righteousness… You are My queen. My thoughts are of good and not evil… You represent Me wherever you go. Face Me; see the pain in My eyes when I see you reveal My holy vessel as a common woman. Please roll over, face Me, and look Me in the eyes! I won't fail you! I won't let you down! Dismount from riding the show horse!"

CHAPTER 5

The Wooden Horse

~~

A re you riding the wooden horse? A wooden horse is dry and barren; it has no feelings left and feels useless. Circumstances in your life have you in despair.

Ruth 1:3-5 (NIV) says, "Now Elimelech, Naomi's husband, died, and she was left with her two sons. They married Moabite women, one named Orpah and the other Ruth. After they had lived there about ten years, both Mahlon and Kilion also died, and Naomi was left without her two sons or her husband." Naomi decided to head back to Judah (Bethlehem). She was so distraught that she changed her name, as evidenced in vv. 20-21: "Call me not Naomi (pleasant); call me Mara (bitter) for the almighty has dealt very bitter with me. I went out full but the Lord brought me empty."

Sometimes terrible things happen to us and we feel God has left us. Yet, in Naomi's deepest despair, God gave her a faithful daughter-in-law, Ruth, who stuck by her. Ruth 1:16-18 says,

"But Ruth replied, 'don't urge me to leave you or to turn back from you. Where you go I will go and where you stay I will stay. Your people will be my people and your God my God. Where you die I will die, and there I will be buried. May the Lord deal with me, be it ever so severely, if anything but death separates you and me.'"

It is hard to imagine that even at your worst, when you feel as though God has forgotten you, someone will see God in your life and be so inspired that they will want to serve Him! Even when you don't feel like your light is shining, someone will see the brightness! I remember when I was being mistreated on my job. I was a Human Resource Consultant and would worked all day then do "in service" presentations for the nurses and doctors evenings. I was being set up to be discouraged to a point where I would give up and quit. While I was going through, others would come to me for encouragement. God will use you while you're in the furnace of affliction to minister to another sister and bless you while you're doing it!

Eventually they laid me off because of "reorganization." I was so hurt, forgetting that God is my source. To make a long story short, when I surrendered the situation to HIM, I got a new revelation! After more than thirty years, God was calling me into full-time ministry. I had to come out of my comfort zone!

Maybe your emptiness is from a circumstance that hurts so badly you can't explain it. Is that how you feel? Do you feel like you can't love, can't witness about God's goodness, can't praise Him? Do you feel like dry wood? Do you say, "Lord, I thirst, I ache, I'm lonely. My sons and daughters have gone astray, I've lost my best friend, my husband divorced me, I'm spiritually dying…"!

I want you to know that even in your deepest despair, if you love God, someone will see God in you. They will believe in your relationship with God so much that they'll say like Ruth said to Naomi, "Where you go, I will go; where you lodge, I will lodge; your people shall be my people and your God my God."

God says, "Your completeness is in Me; lean on Me, trust in Me." Remember, a wooden horse has no vision.

"Where there is no vision, the people perish; but he that keepeth the law, happy is he" (Proverbs 29:18).

In your deepest despair, God will cause you to forget your pain and use you to mentor a "Ruth." He says to us that His thoughts are of good, and not evil. No matter what it looks like, it's working for our good. Romans 8:28 says, "And we know that all things work together for good to them that love God, to them who are the called according to his purpose."

Ruth, who also had her own pain to deal with, was loyal to Naomi. We see her in the fields gleaning. God was working out a plan for her! Ruth 2:1-7 (NIV) says,

Now Naomi had a relative on her husband's side; from the clan of Elimelech, a man of standing, whose name was Boaz. And Ruth the Moabitess said to Naomi, "Let me go to the fields and pick up the leftover grain behind anyone whose eyes I find favor."

Naomi said to her, "Go ahead, my daughter," So she went out and began to glean in the fields behind the harvesters. As it turned out, she found herself working in a field belonging to Boaz, who was from the clan of Elimelech.

Just then Boaz arrived from Bethlehem and greeted the harvesters. "The LORD be with you!" "The LORD bless you!" they called back.

Boaz asked the foreman of his harvesters, "Whose young woman is that?" (Notice that Ruth didn't have to ride the "show horse" to get noticed. Smile.)

The foreman replied, "She is the Moabitess who came back from Moab with Naomi. She said, Please let me glean and gather among the sheaves behind the harvesters. She went into the field and has worked steadily from morning till now, except for a short rest in the shelter."

Note that while you're going through your hardship, you must keep busy. You have no time to waste for pity parties. You can always find someone who spends time complaining and moaning and groaning. But when you know God has a plan, look around you and help others who are in need. Ruth was busy helping someone else through her troubles. While she was putting others before herself, God was busy working out His plan for her life!

Psalm 37:4-5 says, "Delight yourself also in the LORD; and He shall give you the desires of thine heart. Commit thy way unto the LORD; trust also in him; and he shall bring it to pass."

Ruth 4:13-16 continues,

"So Boaz took Ruth and she became his wife. Then he went to her, and the LORD enabled her to conceive, and she gave birth to a son. The women said to Naomi: 'Praise be to the LORD, who this day has not left you without a kinsman redeemer. May he become famous throughout Israel! He will renew your life and sustain you in your old age. For your daughter-in-law, who loves you and who is better to you than seven sons, has given him birth.'" Then Naomi took the child, laid him in her lap, and cared for him. The women living there named him Obed.

Obed was the father of Jesse, the father of David! Ruth's life transformed from empty to full! In the end, God blessed both women more than they could imagine! "Roll over, face Me! For I know the plans I have for you!"

Sarah is another example of a wooden horse. She was dry and barren, both naturally and physically! She and Abram were promised they would be parents. Yet years went by and she never conceived. Finally, she felt she needed to help God! She told her husband to get with her maid, Hagar.

How about you? Are you dry, barren? Are there ministry gifts lying dormant inside of you? Are you doing what God's given you to do or are you looking for a Hagar to do your job? So many of us feel because we've gotten older, we need to help God fulfill the calling He's made on our lives. But we must remember that if God said it, He will perform it against that day!

On the other hand, perhaps you have the "Hagar" mentality. (She bore Ishmael when Abram was eighty-six years old (Gen. 16).) Hagar's just go along with the program; ready for someone else's leftovers. I know she lived in a different culture and was being obedient to her master, but today women are so ready to ride a rented horse! This is a horse borrowed from someone else's stable!

So many women have come to the pillow talk conferences filled with grief because their husbands have left them after 20 years or so, for a younger woman, or a man. (Yes I said "man".) Girlfriend, think about it. Let's get real. If you had him for all those years, those were the best years he had to offer. If you were eating in a plate and years later someone got what was left on the plate, what would they get? Unwanted leftovers! Yes, I know the pain is as real as a death experience, because the relationship has died. If he was a good husband for some of the years he was with you, rejoice over the good times and go on with your life. Become a full-time mentor for a Ruth! Many young women need your experience of being a homemaker! I've experienced it and I can witness to you that life goes on even after he/she leaves!

Hagar's ride is a horse only for a season. "Hagar's" know deep down there's no future—they'll have to give it back when the time is up. If you are a Hagar, ask God to deliver you from thinking so little of yourself that you break up someone else's home to get a man. God has more for you than leftovers.

As we read in Genesis 17:15-16, "And God said unto Abraham, As for Sarai thy wife, thou shalt not call her name Sarai, but Sarah shall be her name. And I will bless her, and give thee a son also of her; yea I will bless her, and she shall be a mother of nations; kings of people shall be of her."

In chapter eighteen we find Sarah laughing at the promise of God. Genesis 18:9-12 says,

"And they said unto him, where is Sarah, thy wife? And he said, Behold, in the tent.

And he said, I will certainly return unto thee according to the time of life; and lo, Sarah thy wife shall have a son. And Sarah heard it in the tent door, which was behind him.

Now Abraham and Sarah were old and well stricken in age; and it ceased to be with Sarah after the manner of women. Therefore Sarah laughed with herself saying,

After I am waxed old shall I have pleasure, my lord being old also?"

Do you see the despair in this situation? Sarah was saying that she and her husband couldn't even find pleasure in each other because their bodies were so old! But I love what verse 14 says: "Is any thing too hard for the LORD? And the time appointed I will return unto thee, according to the time of life, and Sarah shall have a son."

We must understand that a delay does not mean a denial! While we wait for the manifestation of God, we must learn patience, for the promise will come. God cannot lie! Roll over and face HIM!! Genesis 21:1-3 says,

"And the LORD visited Sarah as he had said, and the LORD did unto Sarah as he had spoken. For Sarah conceived, and bore Abraham a son in his old age, at the set time of which God had spoken to him. And Abraham called the name of this son that was born unto him, whom Sarah bore to him, Isaac."

Sarah becomes a mother of nations at ninety-nine years old and Abraham a father at one hundred years old! Face God and surrender your disappointment, your deep hurt, and your sadness. Surrender your family, your wayward children, your son or daughter who is on drugs or incarcerated to a God who has plans for you. You don't have to ride a wooden horse. It is a very uncomfortable position and can lead to many splinters! These are splinters of low self-esteem, fear, and anxiety! Can't you hear His voice softly telling you, "I'll fill your thirst with My living water"?

This just goes to show that God never forgets His promises! He is so close. You can hear Him saying, "Roll over, face me. My thoughts are of good and not evil. My time is not your 24–hour clock. It takes time for Me to groom you. Roll over, face Me. Look in My eyes. Do they look like I would ever forget what I promised you? Do they not tell you I see the struggle you have waiting? Can you see My love for you? Dismount your wooden horse and keep your focus on Me!"

CHAPTER 6

The Racehorse

Maybe you're riding a racehorse or a workhorse. Jesus tells Martha in Luke 10:41-42,

"And Jesus answered and said unto her, Martha, Martha, thou art careful and troubled about many things but one thing is needful and Mary chose that good part which shall not be taken from her."

We read here that Jesus was visiting Mary and Martha. It looked like Mary was letting Martha do all the cooking and cleaning. To other onlookers, you would think Mary was not being fair. Yet when Martha tells Jesus to make Mary help her, Jesus tells her Mary chose to sit at his feet and listen to Him.

Sometimes I feel like Mary, and sometimes I feel like Martha. The stage I am in right now is "Mary." I just want to stay in God's presence and listen to His voice. I desire and hunger for the more of His Word. Yet I remember being busy, while raising the children as a single parent, working full-time, cooking, ironing, doing hair, etc. Many times I feel

I cheated my children out of moments when I was in my bedroom studying my Bible instead of playing games with them.

Do you ever feel frustrated? We are so busy with chores, kids, spouses, jobs, choir rehearsals, prayer meetings, and Bible classes. Are we too busy to spend time with God? You are on a racehorse, running your head off and trying to please everyone. I thought if I could just "do" enough, maybe it would help erase all my sins. There would be no way I could ever pay the penalty for my sins! How dare I try to minimize the bloodshed for the remission of every one of them! The blood of Jesus paid for it all! Romans 5:8-9 says,

> "But God commended his love toward us, in that, while we were yet sinners, Christ died for us. Much more then, being now justified by his blood, we shall be saved from wrath through him." There is no way could I work out my salvation!

God is saying, "Slow down! Face Me; see how I long to spend more time with you." 1 Corinthians 9:24 says,

> "Know ye not that they which run in a race run all, but one receives the prize? So run, that ye may obtain."

About the time I was writing *Pillow Talk*, I received this poem from the computer network. Was it a coincidence? I don't know who wrote it, but it is a powerful poem that ministers to this chapter:

> I knelt to pray, but not for long I had too much to do.

> I had to hurry and get to work for bills would soon be due.

So I knelt and said a hurried prayer,
And jumped up off my knees.
My Christian duty was now done;
My soul could rest at ease.
All daylong I had not time
To spread a word of cheer,
No time to speak of Christ to friends,
They'd laugh at me I'd fear.
No time, no time, too much to do,
That was my constant cry,
No time to give to souls in need
But at last the time to die.
I went before the Lord, I came, I stood with downcast eyes.
For in His hands God held a book;
It was the book of life.
God looked into his book and said
"Your name I cannot find.
I once was going to write it down…
But never found the time."

Remember, a workhorse is needed to plow the fertile ground, lay rows of righteousness straight, and plow the fields of souls in obedience to the master. Laborers are few. Matthew 9:37-38 says,

"Then saith he unto his disciples, The harvest truly is plenteous, but the laborers are few; pray ye therefore the lord of the harvest, that he will send forth laborers into his harvest."

We must quit riding the racehorse! It's moving too fast for intimacy! We must roll over and spend time for intimacy with our Lord and Savior, Jesus Christ!

CHAPTER 7

Horse Drawn Buggy

W hat about the horse drawing the buggy? John 4:4 says,

"He must needs go through Samaria."

You must meet Jesus at the well… The woman who came to the well in John 4:8 thought she came to draw water, but left with more than she came for:

"There cometh a woman of Samaria to draw water: Jesus said unto her, Give me to drink." In verse 9 the woman was so accustomed to being used that she asked a question: "Then said the woman of Samaria unto him, How is it that thou, being a Jew, asks drink of me, which am a woman of Samaria? For the Jews have no dealing with the Samaritans."

When we come to Christ with all our past baggage, He deals with us individually. He heals us individually. He doesn't deal with us according to denomination. Denominations are manmade. God's church is made up of believers who believe Jesus Christ is their Savior and Lord.

Can you imagine what the woman was thinking about all the way to the well? She was probably thinking about the past, revisiting old baggage from past marriages, relationships, hurts, and painful experiences. Maybe she was thinking of her bad marriages or abuse or her old boyfriends. On her way to the well she did not want to face any of the "church folks" who would badmouth her. She was probably thinking, "Let me go to the well when the other townsfolk won't be there." The whole town probably knew of her promiscuity. They knew about her past and all her men.

The first husband may have left her for another woman or another man. Yes, I said *man*. So many marriages are broken up because of homosexuality. The second husband may have beaten her until she finally got tired and left him. The third one may have ended up on drugs or alcohol and landed himself in rehab. No matter how many men she had, there never was a relationship that could satisfy her. There never was a man who could love away her pain. Satisfaction was still not obtained. What happened at the well that day? She met another man, but this time it was different!

I feel so touched by the fact that we can come to Christ and find rest when we are broken, hurt, wounded, and sad. Finally, this woman finds something to quench her thirsty soul. She meets a man who knows her past and, instead of casting her away, ministers to her inner soul.

Verse 16-18 says, "Jesus said unto her, Go, call thy husband, and come hither. The woman answered and said, I have no husband. Jesus said unto her, Thou hast well said, I have no husband: For thou hast had five husbands; and he whom thou now hast is not thy husband; in that said thou truly."

I can relate to this in a way because of my past. When I first came to Jesus, I had already been molested, beaten, divorced, married a second time to a man who already had a wife, and a hopeless sinner. I was dragging all this baggage into my new life with Christ. I found this same water this Samaritan woman speaks about in verse 13-14:

> "Jesus answered and said unto her. Whosoever drinks of this water shall thirst again; but whosoever drinks of the water that I shall give him shall never thirst; but the water that I shall give him shall be in him a well of water springing up into everlasting life."

I shall never forget being filled with the Holy Spirit and having that thirst fulfilled!

> Verse 28-29 says, "The woman then left her water pot, and went her way into the city, and said to the men, come, see a man, which told me all things that ever I did; is not this the Christ?"

Can you imagine the townspeople when they saw this woman? She went to the well that day with a dry and thirsty soul and left an evangelist, compelling men to "come see Jesus." This same Jesus is talking to us today. He is saying to us "Face Me, drop your baggage! Let Me fill you with living water. I'll satisfy where nothing else could! Can't you see My anguish, My compassion, and My love for you? Roll over, face me. Can't you see I can't share you with another lover? You are mine! All the Father gives Me, I lose none. My Spirit dwells in you and I am with you always. I don't like some of the places you take Me. Face me. I want you to hear Me ask you "What are we doing in this place?" Where is your self-respect? My bride, My chosen one, why are we lying in the devil's bed?"

Today, we must deal with what's in the buggy: Is it incest? Homosexual relationships? Abuse? Rejection? Guilt? You may ask yourself these questions: Why is he on drugs/alcohol? What did I do wrong? Why did he leave me for her/him? What does she have that I don't? Listen, it is not about you! Remember, you are the precious jewel!

Unhook the buggy and let it roll down that mountain into destruction. Drop whatever is in your pot and leave it at the well, at the feet of Jesus, today! If you listen carefully, you can hear Jesus whisper to you: "Roll over, Face Me. Face My strength. I won't let you fall. I will under gird you! Give Me your past, your pain from abortions and miscarriages and rejection. Surrender it; I'll give you My future, for I know the thoughts that I have toward you. Now you can minister to that sister who doesn't know Me. Climb under My wings, look in My eyes, and know intimately My healing balm there."

Read Psalm 91:1-14:

"He who dwells in the secret place of the most high shall remain stable and fixed under the shadow of the Almighty [whose power no foe can withstand].

I will say of the Lord, He is my refuge and my Fortress, my God; on Him I lean and rely, and in Him I [confidently] trust! For [then] He will deliver you from the snare of the fowler and from the deadly pestilence. [Then] He will cover you with His pinions, and under His wings shall you trust and find refuge; His truth and His faithfulness are a shield and a buckler. You shall not be afraid of the terror of the night, nor of the arrow (the evil plots and slanders of the wicked) that flies by day, nor of the pestilence that stalks in darkness, nor of the destruction and sudden death that surprises and lay waste at noonday.

A thousand may fall at your side, and ten thousand at your right hand, but it shall not come near you. Only a spectator shall you be [yourself inaccessible in the secret place of the Most High] as you witness the reward of the wicked. Because you have made the Lord your refuge, and the Most High your dwelling place, there shall no evil befall you, nor any plague or calamity come near your tent. For He will give His angels [especial] charge over you to accompany and defend and preserve you in all your ways [of obedience and service]. They shall bear you up on their hands, lest you dash your foot against a stone. You shall tread upon the lion and adder; the young lion and the serpent shall you trample underfoot. Because he has set his love upon Me, therefore I will deliver him; I will set him on high, because he knows and understands My name [has a personal knowledge of My mercy, love and, kindness—trusts and relies on Me, knowing I will never forsake him, no, never]."

"God's thoughts are of good and not evil..." Leave your baggage at the well at the feet of Jesus! Roll over, face God!

CHAPTER 8

Time to Dismount

As long as we are riding a horse and always on the move, we cannot build an intimate relationship. God is calling us to dismount from whatever we're riding so that our relationship is so intimate that our ways become His ways. Isaiah 55:7-9 says,

> "Let the wicked forsake his way, and the unrighteous man his thoughts; and let him return unto the LORD, and he will have mercy upon him; and to our God, for he will abundantly pardon. For my thoughts are not your thoughts, neither are your ways my ways, saith the LORD, For as the heavens are higher that the earth, so are my ways higher than your ways, and my thoughts than your thoughts."

Saul fell to the dirt so that his vision became God's vision. When this happened, Saul's name was changed to Paul and we know today that he became determined and fearless. Even when facing unrelenting persecutions, Paul says in Acts 20:24,

"None of these things move me, neither count I my life dear unto myself so that I might finish my course with joy, and the ministry, which I have received of the Lord Jesus, to testify the gospel of the grace of God."

Paul, writing from prison said (Yes, even from prison you can minister when you have a close relationship with God!) in Philippians 1:6,

"Being confident of this very thing, that he which hath begun a good work in you will perform it until the day of Jesus Christ." This is the same Saul who persecuted Christians. Now, with total transformation, he has an intimacy with God never experienced before! He tells us in Philippians 3: 13-14,

"Brethren, I count not myself to have apprehended; but this one thing I do, forgetting those things which are behind, and reaching forth unto those things which are before, I press toward the mark for the prize of the high calling of God in Christ Jesus."

CHAPTER 9

No More Pacifiers

How will you deal with the pain? No matter how long a baby sucks on a pacifier, there will never be any nourishment going into its belly. The hunger remains. The same thing happens if you continue to cover up a wound and act like it isn't there. The Band-Aid doesn't promote any healing; it just covers up the problem. Are we going to continue to use a Band-Aid even though we know it doesn't heal a wound? Some Band-Aids mentioned in this book are drugs, alcohol, and sex, they are all false pacifiers.

God is telling us its time to quit covering up our mess. The biggest trick Satan uses is telling us no one else is having the same problem and to keep it to ourselves. He tells us not to ask for prayer, because people will talk about us. But when we roll over and face a God who can handle every problem, we no longer have to continue to cover up the problem. No more acting like everything is okay when we know we need to be healed, set free, and delivered. It is time for us to be real. Let's roll over and face a God who knew us before the world began.

This same God does not want us to continue to be broken: "I am come that ye might have life and that they may have it more abundantly" (John 10:10b). Isaiah 61:1-3 says,

"The Spirit of the Lord God is upon me; because the LORD has appointed me to teach good tidings unto the meek; he has sent me to bind up the brokenhearted, to proclaim liberty to the captives, and the opening of the prison to them that are bound; to appoint unto them that mourn in Zion, to give unto them beauty for ashes, the oil of joy for mourning, the garment of praise for the spirit of heaviness; that thy might be called trees of righteousness, the planting of the Lord, that He might be glorified."

It's all about Him being glorified through our lives and not about us! Let's take a trip to The Potter's House and let the healing begin. Jeremiah 18:1-6 says,

"The word, which came to Jeremiah from the Lord, saying, Arise, and go down to the potter's, and there I will cause thee to hear my words.

Then I went down to the potter's house, and, behold, he wrought a work on the wheels.

And the vessel that he made of clay was marred in the hand of the potter: so he made it again another vessel, as seemed good to the potter to make it. Then the word of the LORD came to me, saying, O house of Israel, cannot I do with you as this potter? Saith the Lord. Behold, as the clay is in the potter's hand, so are you in mine hand, O house of Israel."

God never throws the baby out with the bathwater. You are never so lost or so wounded that God can't heal you. But the potter makes you into the vessel that pleases HIM, not you!!

Have you ever had a deep infection? Think about this. The doctor cleans the area with an antiseptic to stave off the germs. He takes a scalpel and lances the wound, or he digs until he reaches the root of the infection. I remember having a fingernail that became ingrown and infected. The doctor continued to dig into the incision unto he reached the heart of the infection. Only when he got deep into the wound could he get all the poison out. It hurt, but no pain, no gain.

God doesn't use a scalpel. Hebrews 4:12 says,

"For the word of God is quick, and powerful, and sharper than any two-edged sword, piercing even to the dividing asunder of soul and spirit, and of the joints and marrow, and is a discerner of the thoughts and intents of the heart."

His Word cuts with a finger of love to expose the deep-rooted hurts, to expose Satan, and to expose that deep-rooted poison of bitterness, unforgiveness, etc. This love hides a multitude of sins. His love is what draws us to the potter's house. Jesus gives us the Word of God, which acts as a scalpel to open up the wound and allow healing to begin!

Ephesians 3:14-16 says, "For this cause I bow my knees to the Father of our Lord Jesus Christ of whom the whole family in heaven and earth is named; that He would grant you according to the riches of His glory to be strengthened with might by His spirit in the inner man."

Our inner man will be healed and strengthened by the spirit of the living God!

After the poison is dug out, the surgeon pours antiseptic solution so that it seeps down deep into the root of the infection to kill the germs. In the spiritual sense, we need an antiseptic that will get to the root of our hurt and pain. Our antiseptic is forgiveness. We must forgive that person who raped us of our childhood. Forgive that person who climbed into your bed when you were a child and had their way with you. Forgive that spouse who abused you, or the parent who abandoned you. Only through the love of Christ can this forgiveness come. We must let forgiveness saturate the wound so it gets the bitterness out. When you forgive through the strength of God, you are getting hatred out. Forgiveness kills the part of us that seeks revenge. "Revenge is mine, saith the Lord, I will repay." We must always remember that God says to us, "I've got a plan and it's a good plan for you."

After the wound has been lanced and the poison dug out, there is a gaping hole. The hole, which is prone to infection, has to be maintained. The doctor has the nurse bathe it two or three times daily and change the dressing regularly to keep the area clean.

The spiritual wound must also be maintained. There is an emptiness after opening the spiritual wound. The wound is prone to infection and susceptible to the works of the enemy. So today we cover it in the blood of Jesus. From this day forward, we will bathe our past in His grace daily. We will do this to clean out pride. Our spiritual gauze will be a dressing of humility and love so that the healing is permanent.

When I look back on the most horrible days of abuse and realize I had not accepted Jesus as my Savior and Lord, it humbles me all the more. To think that He loved me and didn't change His plans for me even when I wasn't living a life pleasing to Him—this is truly a love that surpasses any man's love. I remember getting my gun that my dad mailed to me for protection and desiring to use it to protect my children and myself. But it was not in the plan of God for me to be a murderer. On the day that the kids and I locked ourselves in the bathroom, we were full of fear. We had our backs to the door, trying to keep their father out. It was God's protection that kept me alive that day. God's mercy kept us sane and kept us out of mental institutions.

Their father left the house that day and went to a pay phone to call us. We could hear the phone ringing and ringing, but we were afraid to come out of the bathroom to answer it. It wasn't until later, when their father returned and began to knock on the bathroom door to tell us it was him calling on the phone, did we talk about coming out of that bathroom! Their father said he would leave again and call us to assure us he was no longer in the house. Minutes later, the phone rang. Cecil Jr. was brave enough to leave the bathroom and answer the phone. Once I was told their father was on the other end of the line, we ran to all the windows and doors and secured the locks. We stayed in the same room all night. I can still feel that fear of those days.

Listen, I remember from where God brought me. My pain was so deep that no drugs, sex or alcohol could bring about a permanent solution. I didn't find a permanent solution until I rolled over and faced God. I faced Jesus, who loved me more than I loved myself. I accepted Jesus as my personal Savior, and He changed my whole life. Nobody could love me like Jesus, who died on the cross for my sins before I had committed my first sin! Only He could reach my pain.

CHAPTER 10

It Ain't About Me

$\backsim\!\!\!\backsim$

My sisters and brothers, truly God wants us to be made whole. All of my hurts, past abuse, trouble, and pains have been used as stepping-stones, not stumbling blocks, since my conversion. God works everything for our good and makes our ministries have more substance. If you have no test, you'll have no testimony! I remember feeling that I must be ugly or have something wrong with me if my first husband (now deceased) didn't want me and went with other women. My self-esteem was so low, I blamed myself. After facing God, I learned not only to forgive, but also to realize that he needed to be healed and forgiven just like I did. Only God can make us whole. We must remember it is all about Him, not about us. All through the Bible we find passages telling us that we were created to give Him glory, such as in Ephesians 1:4:

"According as he hath chosen us in him before the foundation of the world, that We should be holy and without blame before him in love; having predestinated us unto the adoption of children by Jesus Christ to himself, according to the good pleasure of HIS will."

It isn't about our will; it's the good pleasure of His will. Quit fighting the inevitable, you must come this way! Roll over and face God.

2 Chronicles 7:14 says, "If my people who are called by my name would humble themselves and pray, and seek my face, and turn from their wicked ways, then will I hear from heaven and forgive their sins and will heal their land."

We are His people! We are the ones called by His name! We must humble ourselves, seek His face, and pray!

When we roll over and face God, we realize how close He is. Don't get me wrong, I knew that once I accepted Jesus as my Savior and was filled with His Spirit, He would never leave me. His spirit dwells in me. However, pillow talk reminds me that He is as close as the other side of my pillow. Instead of keeping my back to Him and drowning myself in my sorrows, I must roll over. When I think about looking into His eyes and seeing the love there, all my doubts are settled.

Ezekiel 37:6, "And I will put sinews on you, make flesh grow back on you, cover you with skin, and put breath in you that you may come alive, and you will know that I am the Lord."

Just like Saul was changed after that day on the Damascus Road, we, too, must be changed. Nothing can take the place of God's presence. We must have a hunger for nothing and no one but Him!

Psalm 42:1-2 (KJV) says, "As the hart panteth after the water brooks, so panteth my soul after thee, O God. My soul thirsteth for God, for the living God; when shall I come and appear before God?" The NIV says, "As the deer pants for streams of water, so my soul pants for you, O God. My soul thirsts for God, for the living God. When can I go and meet with God?"

I say to you roll over; He's right there.

Afterword

My soul hungers for the living God to have fellowship. I had just left a women's retreat where I spoke three times, and the presence of the Lord was still with me in the car. It was so strong I just wanted to stop and bask in the intimacy. I could hear Him say in my spirit, "This is Pillow talk". It meant intimacy with God. A relationship bringing me closeness beyond what I could have with any human being. It was frightening, in a way. You see, I always thought of "pillow talk" in a cheap way because of movies and the world's way of thinking. Yet God was demanding intimacy. He wanted me to seek Him with every part of my being!

I kept thinking about Jeremiah 29:11-14. The NIV translation says,

> "For I know the plans I have for you," declares the LORD, "plans to prosper you and not to harm you, plans to give you hope and a future. Then you will call upon me and come and pray to me, and I will listen to you. You will seek me and find me when you seek me with all your heart."

I know part of me can't be seeking after things of my flesh. Let's face it. If part of our heart is seeking out Jodi, Harry or Mary; riches, fame or prestige, then the seeking is not with all our heart. The Word of God continues to say, "I will be found by you says the Lord, and I will restore your fortunes and gather you from all the nations and all the places where I have driven you...and I will bring you back to the place from which I sent you into exile." It's like He is talking directly to me, saying, "Call Me out of a vital necessity, and find Me when you search for Me with all your heart!" Pillow Talk is intimacy with God as we roll over and face HIM!

Other products by Evangelist Shiela Austin Jones

Book: Made Whole in the Potter's Hands:
Co-written by Shiela Austin Jones and Earnestine F. Grigler Jeffers

CD's
"Evangelist Shiela Austin Jones Sings"

"Reaping the Harvest for the Kingdom"

"Pillow Talk"
(Pillow Talk CD includes the message "Pillow Talk" and songs sung by Evangelist Shiela Jones)

Pillows
"Pillow Talk" Pillows
(with scripture Jeremiah 29:11)

About the Author

⌒

Evangelist Shiela Jones is truly a spirit-filled woman of God. She is licensed and ordained, and she preaches and sings with conviction that our lives should pattern the holy life of Jesus Christ. Her well-known message "Pillow Talk" has brought healing to thousands through the anointing on her life.

She has co-authored a book, *Made Whole in the Potter's Hand*. The book tells of many miracles God has done in her life while she was a single parent. The greatest miracle is a transformed life from sin to a sanctified life in Christ Jesus. Truly, old things are passed away and behold all things become new!

As a gospel songwriter and recording artist, she recorded a single titled "He's in This Place" with the James Greer Singers; two albums, "I'll Die for Him" with the Voices of Deliverance and "My God is In Control" with One Way Records. Her latest CD's; "Broken Vessel" and "Shiela Austin Jones Sings" have received rave reviews from the vast supporters of her ministry..

Evangelist Jones is the founder of H.U.G. (Holiness Unto God) Ministries, which uses Romans 12:1 as its motto: "Present your body Holy and acceptable unto God, which is your reasonable service." Her television show, *Decisions*, aired every Sunday morning on WJYS in Chicago for two years.

She has a heart for people and reaches out to all while preaching and singing for churches and organizations of all denominations. She was featured twice as guest speaker and soloist in Madrid, Spain, once for the United States Air Force. She also ministers to souls in prisons, mental health centers, nursing homes, retreats, and seminars.

Evangelist Jones and her supportive husband, Philip attend the Apostolic Church of God in Chicago, Illinois. Their pastor is Bishop Arthur M. Brazier.

Printed in the United States
79601LV00002B/1-375